Successfu!
Public
Relations
in a week

Claire Austin

 eadway · Hodder & Stoughton

British Library Cataloguing in Publication Data

Austin, Claire
  Successful Public Relations in a week.– (Headway business in a week)
  I. Title   II. Series
  659.2

ISBN 0 340 56479 2

First published 1992

Impression number 10 9 8 7 6 5 4 3 2
Year   1999 1998 1997 1996 1995 1994
Typeset by Multiplex Techniques Ltd, St Mary Cray, Kent
Printed in Great Britian for Hodder & Stoughton Educational, a
division of Hodder Headline Plc., 338 Euston Road, London
NW1 3BH by St. Edmundsbury Press, Bury St. Edmunds, Suffolk.

C O N T E N T S

the *Institute*
of *Management*

F O U N D A T I O N

The Institute of Management (IM) is at the forefront of management development and best management practice. The Institute embraces all levels of management from students to chief executives. It provides a unique portfolio of services for all managers, enabling them to develop skills and achieve management excellence.

For information on the benefits of membership, please contact:

Department HS
Institute of Management
Cottingham Road
Corby
Northants NN17 1TT

Tel: 0536 204222
Fax: 0536 201651

This series is commissioned by the Institute of Management Foundation.

A squirrel is just a rat with good public relations!

Public relations (PR) is an often misunderstood and undervalued management tool.

To many it is seen as just another form of advertising while others dismiss PR as dealing with journalists and sending out press releases.

In fact, it can play a central role in the achievement of specific objectives at all levels of an organisation's work, by focusing, reinforcing and communicating an effective message.

Used properly, public relations is an excellent and cost-effective method of improving the image of an individual, organisation or product. It is about ensuring that your audience receives, and accepts, the message you wish to project.

Public relations involves many other disciplines and it can have an impact on every aspect of an organisation. It is about projecting the right message and as such, it can involve press relations, advertising, marketing, sponsorship, exhibitions, local community events, the environment and public affairs.

The world of PR can seem baffling to the outsider but it shouldn't do. Much of the PR role is basic and straightforward. It doesn't have to cost a fortune either. Many successful PR operations exist on tiny budgets. To do so they have to define their aims clearly and ration their resources.

■ I N T R O D U C T I O N ■

Communication is the key to public relations –
communicating the right message to the public, employees,
shareholders and other specific target audiences.

This book aims to give you ' the non PR specialist ' an
understanding of what public relations can do for you and
your organisation. It will also arm you with the basic tools
for conducting your own PR programme.

Over the next seven days we will be looking at the role PR
plays in an organisation. We will also examine media
relations and by the end of the week you will be confident
about writing effective press releases, television and radio
interviews and coping with bad news.

 Public relations is:

* Projecting the right message
* Cost-effective
* An excellent management tool

About PR

Today we shall examine the purpose of public relations,
highlighting some of the benefits to be gained. We will
separate the myths surrounding PR from the facts and look
at how the operation is usually managed.

- PR defined
- Why use PR?
- Benefits
- Myths and facts
- How PR is usually managed

PR defined

The Institute of Public Relations (IPR) defines public
relations as:

'the planned and sustained effort to establish and

maintain goodwill and mutual understanding between
an organisation and its publics'

Why use PR?

Individuals and organisations can survive without PR, but
with a planned PR programme they can expect better results
and an enhanced reputation.

Obviously no amount of good public relations can hide a
bad product or protect an unethical company. For public
relations to succeed the organisation must be *credible*. PR
alone can't cure a terminally sick organisation. What it can
do is help to promote a positive image and to minimise the
damage which occurs when something does go wrong.

What happens if you don't use PR?

No matter how good you are, if you don't communicate
with your publics, you won't put your messages across. You
will lose out to your rivals who are using public relations
more aggressively to ensure effective communication.

All organisations can benefit from PR. Even a monastery of
trappist monks relies on good PR of some form to ensure it
continues to attract would-be novices, and in its dealings
with the local community.

It is not possible to abdicate from a public image. If you are
not managing the information by which people form their
opinions, their view of you will be based solely on what
they hear from other sources.

You can't quantify what you lose if you don't use PR but companies which do use it can see the benefits in increased awareness of themselves and their products; better staff recruitment and retention; greater market share; customer loyalty and shareholder satisfaction. In other words it helps them operate more successfully on all levels of business.

Benefits

Many people believe they don't need PR because they are ignorant of what it can do for them.

Excuses include:

- 'We're already working to full capacity. If we talked to the press we would only stimulate extra demand which we couldn't handle.'
- 'If we don't say anything we can't be misquoted. Journalists only twist what you say anyway.'
- 'It's just another form of advertising.'
- 'We're not a public company so we don't need public relations.'

But cultivating a good public relations image is worthwhile and having a bad image in the eyes of the public can have disastrous consequences.

All organisations have customers – whatever their business. Those customers might not fit into an easy pigeon hole because the organisation might not manufacture a product, but there will still be customers.

Examples of customers include people who buy products or services; shareholders; client contacts; suppliers – from bank managers to office furniture makers – and last, but not least, employees and prospective employees.

A manufacturing company's customers are the people who buy its products; a hotel's customers are the people who stay in it; the customers of a hospital include the patients and the GPs who refer them; a local authority's customers are the people who live in its catchment area and use its services; a trade association's customers are its members; and a newspaper's customers are its readers, advertisers and the people whose deeds are reported within its pages.

In order to operate effectively and efficiently an organisation needs to recognise and meet the needs of all its customers – some more obvious than others.

This means
- identifying all potential customers
- identifying and responding to their needs
- communicating with them

Identifying your customers

- Where do your customers come from?
- Who buys your products?
- Who is your main rival? Is its reputation better than yours?
- Where do you recruit your staff from?
- Do you find it easy to recruit high quality staff?

Responding to customer needs

- What do your customers want from you?
- What do you provide that your rivals don't, i.e. what is your unique selling point (USP)?

Communicating with your customers

- How do your customers hear about you?
- Are you quoted in the press more or less frequently than your rivals?
- Do you monitor your advertising to ensure it really is effective?
- What do your employees think of your organisation?

If an organisation answers these questions satisfactorily then it will learn about all its customers and benefit rapidly from an improved public image. The process of reviewing communication in an organisation is often referred to as a *communications audit*.

Each type of customer will need a different approach.

Potential buyers of goods or services will want to know that what they are buying is reliable, will do what it claims to and is competitively priced. Potential suppliers will need to be confident that you are a reliable organisation, that you are financially stable and that you will pay your bills on time. Shareholders will only want to invest money in your organisation if they believe it will give them a good return. Many are now also taking a keen interest in a company's ethics, particularly with regard to the environment. Employees and potential employees will want to know the organisation is secure and that it has a good reputation for taking care of its staff.

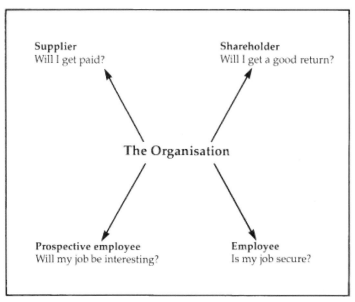

To test your current image you can carry out some easy market research. Go into the local town, pretend to be a stranger and ask 20 different people for directions on how to find your organisation. Ask strangers in the pub, garage or library and try to gain some idea of what image they have of your company.

- Who knows about you?
- Do they know where you are?
- Do they know what you do?
- Do they have a favourable impression of your organisation?

The results of this basic market research could prove most enlightening. Each person you speak to could be a potential customer. If they don't know about you – or worse if they have an unfavourable impression of you – they represent missed opportunities and lost customers.

Myths and facts

Myth	Fact
PR is organised lying.	PR is about presenting a positive image, not a false one.
Nobody believes what is written in the press.	People take much more notice of and are willing to believe a news story if it is printed in the main body of a paper, than an advert, no matter how glossy the advert is.
It's a waste of money.	Used properly and to complement other parts of an organisation's activities, PR can actually save money.
Companies that are doing well don't need PR.	All companies, regardless of their current performance, benefit from PR. A good public relations image built up in the good years can help see a company through the darker, bleaker periods. A poor public image is a handicap which can take a company years to overcome.

It's the gin and tonic brigade.

PR is about more than just cultivating contacts. It is about devising and implementing strategic campaigns, reacting to crises as they happen and ensuring the organisation is always correctly represented.

How PR is usually managed

Regardless of the size of an organisation, public relations is either handled in-house by employees or by an external agency on a consultancy basis.

Whichever route, it is important that someone senior is given responsibility for public relations. In a small organisation that might be the managing director while in a multi-national company the PR function is likely to be handled by a specialist director.

Whoever is responsible for the day-to-day running of the department, it is vital that it has the support of top management. In many of the UK's leading companies the chairman or chief executive, who understands the true value of effective public relations, takes a personal interest in it and ensures it receives the support and commitment of the rest of the board.

In-house teams have the following advantages

- They really know the business
- They have no conflicting loyalties
- They are on the scene when stories break
- They have access to the chairman and others who make key decisions affecting the company's future

On the other hand, external agencies have the following advantages:

- They usually have greater staff resources
- They can sometimes find it easier to deliver unwelcome advice because they are detached from the organisation
- They have a more flexible workforce for dealing with specialist projects

There are no hard and fast rules about what is best. Each organisation and each situation is different. This book does not set out to recommend either the agency or in-house route. Instead it aims to equip every manager with the basic tools of PR and the confidence to manage their own public relations.

Summary

Why should you use PR?

Use PR because:

- It creates a good image
- It makes people more keen to do business with you
- It improves your standing in the local community
- It makes it easier to attract, and retain, a high calibre workforce
- It puts you in the press when you want to be there
- It works!

Action for the day

Carry out a basic market research exercise to find out about your company's reputation in the local vicinity.

Go into town and ask 20 different people – taxi drivers, bus drivers, librarians, publicans, garage attendants, etc – for directions on how to find your offices. Then think about these questions:

- Do they know where your offices are?
- Do they know what your company does?
- Do they know anything about you?
- What impression do they have of your company?

PR and the company

Public relations is generally regarded as part of an organisation's marketing strategy. It complements and enhances advertising programmes, direct mail campaigns, publicity material, corporate literature and the organisation's overall corporate identity.

Today we will be examining what constitutes the marketing mix, how PR affects each element of that mix and the importance of corporate identity. We will also look at what constitutes news and we will explain how to identify the main media for your purposes. Finally we will look at the different ways of getting information printed in the press and at establishing a press office.

- What is the marketing mix?
- How does PR affect the mix?
- Corporate identity
- How important is corporate identity?
- What is news?
- Which media?
- How to get into print
- The press office

There is no sharp line between marketing and public relations. Traditionally people have been keen to divide marketing into separate segments and to treat each function on its own. But this is too rigid a formula. PR affects every aspect of an organisation and as such should be treated as an integral part of all the organisation's activities and functions.

What is the marketing mix?

This has been referred to as the Four Ps – product, price, place and promotion.

- Product – the commodity or service being supplied
- Price – this defines its quality and its market positioning
- Place – where it is available and how it is distributed
- Promotion – how it is sold to the customer

How does PR affect the mix?

Public relations is about ensuring the right messages are presented to the public. These messages can be about a product with regard to:

- Its performance
- The company and its ethics
- The financial health of a company
- Its reputation as a good and caring employer

Although organisations can exist without public relations, those that use PR effectively will find it easier to sell their products, recruit and retain staff and deal with suppliers.

PR complements all elements of a business, but especially the other marketing functions. Good PR will help create a positive image of a product, which in turn will encourage the market to search it out (aid distribution); make customers value it more (support the price); and encourage them to show it to friends (boost promotion).

Communication lies at the heart of public relations and PR can be used as a direct advertising tool.

One example of this is the series of Nescafé Gold Blend advertisements which focus on the relationship between a glamorous couple who drank that particular brand of coffee. The adverts followed the relationship from the first meeting to an eventual – and much publicised – kiss.

Although undoubtedly a strong series of adverts, much of the success has been due to the public relations activity which centred on the 'will they, won't they' angle between the featured couple. The free comment and articles in national newspapers on the screen kiss were worth far more in advertising terms than the comparatively small amount spent on public relations.

Similarly direct mail can be enhanced by previous PR activity. Someone who receives a letter from a company they have already heard about and whose image is positive is much more likely to respond favourably and less likely to put the letter in the bin, than if they receive a letter from an

organisation they have either not heard of or whose reputation is poor.

People are much more likely to believe what they read in the body of a newspaper or magazine than what is written in an advert on the facing page. PR can persuade editors and journalists to write about a product, thereby giving it free editorial publicity, which in turn will be read by potential customers.

The line between free editorial publicity and an advertising puff is very thin. No journalist is going to write about a product just because the PR person wants them to. They need to be persuaded that there is an angle, something that makes the product newsworthy. It could be that:

- The product is revolutionary in some way
- It uses a completely new manufacturing process
- It has already been ordered by a major customer – the more unusual the better
- It marks a significant milestone in the company's history, for example the millionth produced

Whatever it is will help you persuade the newspaper that your product is worth writing about.

Corporate identity

Corporate identity is all about your company's image. It doesn't just concern expensive advertising campaigns. Instead it embraces all those areas which interface with the public. This can include your buildings, transport fleet, literature, letter headings and staff.

One of the most important and instantly recognisable pieces of company literature is the annual report. The annual report is an excellent PR tool. Once a year it is the company's chance to communicate with the public. As well as sending it to shareholders it should also be given to staff and the media. With this in mind it is vital that it adheres to the corporate image of the organisation.

Some companies spend millions on establishing and maintaining a cohesive corporate identity, believing it to be a shrewd investment. Recent examples of companies which have altered their corporate image include BT, BP and ICI.

Consider your company's image. Does it reflect what you really want to present? Do you see your company as dynamic, reliable, solid, trustworthy, world class, or offering good value, and does your image fit this?

First impressions mean a lot. A good name and a strong reputation can take years to build up but the public gains an instant image of what your company is really like when they first come into contact with it. This contact can be by:

- Telephone
- Personal visit
- Buying your products
- Using your services

So it is important that all these areas fit your corporate image.

What is the image of your employees?

When someone rings your company are they greeted courteously and dealt with efficiently, or are they left hanging on the end of the telephone or misrouted and left with the impression that no one seems to want their custom?

What about the employees who come into visual contact with customers? Are they a good advertisement for your company? Do they have smart, easily recognisable uniforms? Are they proud of their appearance? Similarly what are your offices like? Is the car park free from puddles and potholes? Potential customers and suppliers will not be impressed if they have to wade through muddy water to reach you.

What about your products or services. Do you always meet delivery targets? What percentage of goods are returned because they are faulty? How many of your customers come back time and time again?

Public relations can enhance a company's image, but it cannot make up for poor quality goods or unreliable service. It is no good spending thousands of pounds on expensive advertising campaigns if you are unable to deliver products on time.

Similarly, although you might have an excellent repair service wouldn't it be better to get things right the first time? That way you wouldn't need to spend so much on repairing or replacing faulty goods and your reputation for providing good reliable products would improve dramatically.

The most obvious symbol of corporate identity is the company logo.

The logo embodies the image of an organisation in concentrated form. It can be used to carry a positive image throughout an organisation and into its markets in a cheap and effective manner. It can be incorporated in all literature, on company vehicles, employee uniforms, at the head office and on all products. The aim of the logo is to provide instant recognition that something belongs to your organisation. Simple logos are best. Some of the most successful corporate logos are very simple ideas – consider those of Shell, the Prudential Corporation and Jaguar.

But remember, the logo must get across the image and message you want – a poor image can be communicated just as effectively as a good one!

When choosing a logo you should pick something that reflects, in a positive way, the overall image of your company. Keep it simple, easy to reproduce and to recognise. Once you have chosen it, enforce it, ensure that all your employees in every branch office – no matter how far away – use it.

How important is corporate identity?

The simple answer is *very*. A strong, positive corporate identity can enhance your company across all its operations, while a poor identity will be equally effective in weakening your reputation. A good image can take years to build, but it can be quickly tarnished by negative publicity. Great care is needed to foster and protect an organisation's reputation.

A strong corporate identity results in people trusting in the value of you and your products. They are happy to deal with you and give you their custom. They will come back to you time and time again – you gain their loyalty. Your reputation is enhanced and this in turn helps to reinforce your corporate identity.

What is news?

News is something that someone, somewhere doesn't want printed.

News is also what ordinary people want to read about.

News about you and your company can be about new products, developments, buildings, charitable fund raising, sponsorship activities, financial results, employee activities or any other activity which 'the man on the Clapham omnibus' would like to know about.

Before you can start to discover which of your company's activities are newsworthy you need to work out who your target audience is. Who do you want to read about your activities?

To define your target audience ask yourself who you are trying to reach. If you are trying to reach shareholders your target is the readers of the city and business pages of the quality nationals. If you are trying to reach potential employees you need to concentrate on the local press and the specialist journals for your industry.

Once you have identified the target audience you can start identifying what is of interest to them and which are the right media.

How do you define what would be of interest to your target audience?

Read your local newspapers and specialist trade magazines – the ones you have targeted as being most appropriate for your key audiences.

- What interests them?
- What stories are they writing about?
- What sort of items do they cover?
- Which of your activities are likely to appeal to them?

Which media?

There are:

- Newspapers – both local and national and don't forget the freesheets which have massive circulations
- Magazines – consumer, specialist and trade
- Radio and television – not forgetting satellite and cable channels

The choice is endless but it is up to you to select the most appropriate for your needs.

To start with, don't try to cover too many publications and stations. You can't hope to contact everyone and what you have to say will only be of interest to a small selection anyway.

Concentration is often the secret of success.

To begin with you should select no more than six – the six most relevant to you and your company. In this way you can focus your resources in those areas which are most likely to generate results.

Examine your potential target media. Compare the different ways that newspapers tackle the same story. For example contrast the angle *The Sun* takes over a story with that taken by *The Times*. Look at the way the trade and specialist press handles stories – often giving them more room and covering them in greater depth than the national press is able to.

How to get into print

There are four ways of getting into print.

1   Issuing a press release
2   Writing an article
3   Writing a letter to a newspaper
4   Giving a printable quote to a journalist

The most commonly used method is writing a *press release* and we will be examining how to write one on Wednesday. However, with a press release you cannot guarantee it will be printed. News editors receive hundreds of press releases every day. Most are unusable because they are either poorly targeted or they are not newsworthy. Others don't contain enough information or confuse news with views and therefore are not suitable for publication. When writing a press release your task is to ensure it:

* is newsworthy
* is correctly targeted
* covers all the relevant information
* is written in a journalistic style

Even if you follow all these rules you still cannot guarantee publication because at the end of the day your story is fighting for space with vast numbers of other stories. It is a fact of life for journalists that many of their stories are *spiked* (not printed) and never see the light of day. So you cannot, and should not, expect everything you send out to be used.

Some newspapers and trade magazines will accept articles for publication. Often these accompany advertising features and a common example is of an article written by an estate

agent to complement a property advertising feature. Rules about how to write articles for publication are outlined on Wednesday.

A letter for publication has a better statistical chance of being published than a press release. The letter can be commenting on an article printed earlier in the paper or it can comment on some aspect of your business – for instance, if you have raised money for charity and have written a press release which wasn't published you can write a letter for publication which praises the efforts of your employees.

To have your comments in the press you can either be *proactive* or *reactive*. To be proactive you need to ring the newspaper or magazine and to have either a strong view on something which has already been published, or a local angle to a national story. Although you are just as likely to be met with a polite rebuttal as for your views to be printed, it is well worth trying this course of action. By doing so, you will also get yourself known and are likely to be approached by the journalist when they are looking for a local view on a subject.

The press office

If you are going to take public relations seriously you should consider establishing your own press office. Staffing obviously depends on the size of your company and the value you put on a public relations programme, but the minimum required is a press/public relations officer with secretarial support.

The duties of the press officer include:

- Liaison with the media
- Monitoring the media
- Identifying company events which could be publicised
- Distributing press releases

The press officer will need to have the confidence of the senior staff. He or she must have access to all parts of the company's business in order to operate efficiently. They will be unable to perform their jobs properly if they don't have access to all parts of the business and instead have to rely on information being passed down.

Communication is vital for the efficient running of the press office. Ideally the office should be established at the company's headquarters to ease communication with senior staff. Consideration should also be given to installing a direct line phone so that the media do not have to negotiate the company switchboard.

They will also need to have access to up-to-date media lists (Sources of information are dealt with on Saturday).

Summary

- PR is an important part of the marketing mix
- PR affects every aspect of a company's business
- A strong corporate identity is essential
- News is what people want to read about
- You and your company can make the news
- Identifying the right media is vital
- Anyone can get into print if they follow basic rules

Action for the day

Compare and contrast how different newspapers treat the same story. Look at a popular tabloid (*Sun*, *Daily Mirror*, *Star*, *Today*), a more upmarket tabloid (*Daily Mail*, *Daily Express*) and a quality newspaper (*Guardian*, *Times*, *Daily Telegraph*, *Independent*, *Financial Times*) and compare the way they each report the same story. Now consider these questions:

- Who gives it the most coverage?
- What angle are they taking?
- Are politics involved?

Then compare the treatment the same story is given in the trade press.

PR and the press

Today we shall be concentrating on how to deal with journalists. We will look at the various types of journalists and we will examine the dos and don'ts of dealing with the media. We will find out how to run a press conference and uncover some of the jargon used by those in the media.

- How to deal with journalists
- Which journalists should you be dealing with?
- How to make contact with journalists
- So you've got a story to tell
- The interview
- The press conference
- Jargon

How to deal with journalists

Journalists and reporters come in all shapes and sizes, from the youngest cub reporter on a local weekly newspaper to the editor of the *Sunday Times* or presenter of a television current affairs programme. Although all their jobs are different, they have one thing in common – the desire to uncover a big story.

Journalists have to be jacks of all trades. The nature of their jobs means they have to report on a myriad of events and cannot hope to be an expert on every topic they cover. Even a specialist correspondent will admit to being less confident about reporting some facts than others. And this is where you come in. You are an expert in your particular field or specialism. You are in a strong position because you are able to give the journalist the benefit of your experience and can make his or her job easier.

Journalists rely on experts such as yourself to lead them through technical minefields and to enable them to gain an understanding of their subject so that they can write a good article.

The reputation of journalists is little higher than that of time share salesmen. They are believed to be hard drinking, heavy smoking individuals whose desire to get a story outweighs all other considerations. They will walk all over people and don't mind who gets hurt along the way as long as they get their exclusive.

This is an unfair reputation. Most reporters are decent, respectable people who want to report accurately and who

value the contacts they make in the course of their investigations. Often, they are sent by their news editor to cover a story which they know little about and do not understand. Be patient with them. Help them as much as you can and you will be rewarded with a favourable write-up.

The majority also live in the community they are reporting on. They are part of that community and they know that if they upset people it will become harder and harder for them to do their jobs.

Which journalists should you be dealing with?

Newspapers, magazines and the broadcast media all have their own hierarchies. At the bottom of the ladder – and your most likely contact point – is the journalist or reporter.

Journalist/reporter

There are two categories of journalist/reporter, the specialist and the general reporter.

Most start as a general reporter. Their job is to write on any given topic. Often they cover a geographical area for a newspaper and they are responsible for reporting on everything that happens within it – from flower shows to murders, with your company's open day, record profits or new building plans somewhere in the middle. Most weekly newspapers have a number of general reporters. Provincial daily and national newspapers and magazines also have large numbers of general reporters.

As a general rule journalists and reporters are not responsible for the headlines which accompany their articles. A common complaint from the public is that the headline 'gave a false impression' of what the story was about. This is often due to the sub editor – the headline writer – having to think up a headline without having time to read the whole story. Instead they have to rely on the first few paragraphs which can lead to misrepresentation.

Specialist reporters tend to be found on larger weekly newspapers or on daily newspapers – both national and local. They cover a specific topic – education, business, crime, etc.

Chief reporter

This is the most senior journalist in the newsroom and he or she will normally have the pick of all the best stories.

News editor

The news editor is responsible for news selection. He or she decides which items the paper should be covering and which reporter should cover them. The news editor keeps the news diary and is responsible for deciding which stories should be on each page of the newspaper, what the front page lead – the main story – should be and which stories should be accompanied by photographs.

Sub editor

The sub editors are responsible for page layout, headlines and the look of the paper. They don't write the stories themselves, they amend stories written by journalists. Headline writing is an art. Headlines cannot just be any collection of words, they have to fit a given space and they must grab the reader's attention.

Editor

The editor has ultimate control of and responsibility for the tone, style and content of the newspaper. He or she rarely writes news items although is often responsible for the opinion column in those papers which have one. The editor's role is often a managerial one.

How to make contact with journalists

To find out who you should be contacting, ring the newspaper and ask to speak to the news editor. Explain who you are, what you and your company do and ask the news editor to put you in touch with the most appropriate journalist.

Once you have identified who you should be speaking to, ring them up, introduce yourself and arrange a meeting at which you can brief the reporter about your company, the extent of your knowledge and how you can help them in the future. You do not have to arrange an expensive media lunch, just invite them to come to your company to have a look round, or offer to meet them in their own office.

Although journalists have a reputation for liking to be wined and dined they have jobs to do and they have the same pressures on their time as any other individual. If their deadline is early afternoon they will find it hard to get away over lunch and they will appreciate meeting you at a more convenient time.

Most journalists will be happy to attend such a meeting with you. They are always keen to make new contacts and they will not be expecting a story from you – what they want is to know how you can help them in the future.

Once you have made contact and had a face to face meeting, it will be much easier to ring up in the future with a story.

Before the meeting, spend some time doing your homework. Read some of the articles the journalist has written and at your meeting comment favourably on them. Flattery has never harmed anyone.

A note of caution – journalists change jobs frequently and it can be frustrating to build up a good rapport with a local journalist only to find that he or she has moved on to another paper and you have to start all over again. There is no way round it and it can be beneficial because the local journalist you once nurtured as a contact could end up as editor of the *Sunday Times* and once your name is in their contact book, it will stay there.

So you've got a story to tell

Before ringing the contact you have already made, jot down on a piece of paper the main points you wish to put across. In that way you won't forget any important piece of information.

Make sure you can talk confidently about the subject and that you have all the relevant facts at your fingertips. If you are ill-prepared and cannot answer some of the questions the journalist puts to you, you will not make a very favourable impression.

Think about the *timing*. Find out what the relevant deadline is. All newspapers have deadlines and journalists are less likely to be friendly towards you if you ring them just before their deadline.

Each newspaper has a different deadline but as a general rule the deadline for an evening newspaper is about 10am and for a morning paper it is 6pm the previous evening. On a weekly paper the deadline is usually sometime the day before.

The deadline is for the front page only. All the other pages will already have *gone to bed* (be ready for printing) so unless your story really is front page material it won't make that edition if you leave it until the last minute. As a general rule get your story to the paper as early as possible in order to have the greatest chance of having it printed.

The interview

How can you be sure that what you say will be reported accurately and that the reporter won't put words in your mouth? You can't, but you can take certain steps.

1 You can record the interview. Ask the journalist in advance if he or she minds you recording the interview.

Most will have no qualms and you will be left with hard proof of what you actually said.

2   You can ask to see the article before it is printed. Very few journalists will agree to this unless they want to check some very detailed technical information.

3   You can ask for any direct quotes to be phoned over to you before the article is printed. Many journalists – although not all – are willing to do this.

The press conference

Journalists are often happy to attend an event – the laying of a foundation stone, presentation of a cheque to a local charity, launch of a new product, etc. This can be arranged solely for them, in which case it is called a press conference, or they can be invited along with other guests.

Whichever you choose, there are certain rules you should follow.

1   Make the press welcome. Arrange a press table or reserve seats for the press where they can see and hear clearly. Journalists like to have a table to rest their notebooks on, but if this isn't possible they can do without. They are also often keen to sit near an exit so that they can slip away unobtrusively if they have to leave to cover another story.

2   Arrange for the press to have access to a telephone. If your story is important enough or if your press conference is being held just before the newspaper's deadline the journalist might need to phone the story through to the news desk in order to meet the deadline.

3 Offer refreshments. This doesn't have to be a sit-down,
   three course lunch – in fact most journalists would
   rather give that a miss because it takes up too much
   time and they will have to leave before the pudding if
   not the main course! A cup of coffee and biscuits, or
   sandwiches and a glass of wine will be sufficient.

4 Ensure your company representatives can stay after
   the conference to take questions from journalists on a
   one-to-one basis. Many journalists prefer to ask
   questions after a press conference rather than during
   the conference itself. In that way they keep their line of
   questioning – and therefore the angle they are taking –
   hidden from their rivals on other papers.

5 Arrange for press packs to be distributed to everyone at the press conference. A press pack should contain all the information a journalist needs. A typical pack could contain a press release, background information on the release – i.e. technical details of a new product, the latest annual report, a list of company contact names and phone numbers, and photographs if appropriate. Press packs should also be sent to all those journalists who could not attend the press conference.

6 If there are likely to be photo opportunities make sure that photographers are able to move around freely and that your company representatives are aware that their photographs could be taken during the press conference.

The format of a typical press conference would be for the chief executive, chairman or other company representative to make a short presentation, using visual aids if appropriate, and then to call for questions from the assembled journalists. The presentation should not be too long or too detailed.

Jargon

No comment

Never use this phrase. Most journalists take it to mean that whatever they have just asked you is true. It is much better to give a proper answer and if you really don't have any information or opinion on a subject explain that it is outside your interest/role and therefore you are unable to help.

Off the record

This means that what you tell a journalist is true but you are not prepared to be quoted. Many people misuse the phrase, tell the reporter something 'off the record' believing it to be confidential and are then dismayed when they are quoted in the paper. The simple rule is that if you don't want a journalist to know something, don't tell him or her. A journalist does not have to abide by the unwritten 'off the record' rule.

For background information

If you want to give a journalist a steer in the right direction without giving the full facts you can use this phrase. It enables you to give some information but will force the journalist to go elsewhere for confirmation.

Summary

- Journalists rely on people like you – to provide them with stories
- You are the expert – journalists will value your opinion
- Don't miss deadlines
- Treat all journalists the same – you never know who will end up editing a national newspaper
- Never say *No comment*

Action for the day

Prepare a one-page background briefing paper on your organisation for a journalist.

It should be informative about your company and you should answer the following questions:

- What is the nature of your business?
- How many people do you employ?
- How long have you been trading?
- How long have you been in your current location?
- Who is your chief executive?
- Where can they get more information?

The press release

Today we will be looking at getting yourself known. We will learn the basic steps for self-promotion and we will concentrate on how to write a press release and the use of photography.

- Promoting yourself
- How to write a press release
- When to send a press release
- Using photography effectively

Promoting yourself

You can set yourself up as an authoritative spokesman for your industry/organisation. All it takes is a little time and some legwork. Firstly you have to decide what your position is.

- What are *you* uniquely able to comment on?
- In what way are you/is your company different?
- What is your specialism?
- What are you an authority on?

For instance, you might be in a small packaging business. You are both a manufacturer and a small business – either of which you could use for self-promotion. Or you might be the personnel manager of a company which manufactures defence products. You could therefore be an authority on all aspects of employment law, recruitment problems, absenteeism, working conditions as well as on matters connected with defence including arms talks, defence cuts and supplying arms to Third World countries.

You need to search out opportunities for self-promotion. No one is going to come to you, you have to go to them.

One of the best ways to promote yourself is to use the letters to the editor column in newspapers and specialist magazines. If they have carried an article which you believe you can comment on write to the editor, marking your letter 'For Publication'. Your letters will not always be printed but a significant proportion could well be.

You can also offer to write articles for the media. Your offer is unlikely to be accepted by national newspapers which are inundated with offers, but local and specialist media are often interested in receiving articles from informed sources.

Do not expect to be paid for these articles. You are doing it for publicity and promotion, not financial reward.

If you are asked to write an article you should construct it in the same way that you would write a press release, as outlined later in this chapter. Write in the style of the newspaper, using short sentences, avoiding superfluous words and keeping the language simple. Write the required number of words only. If you have been asked for 1000 words don't write 1500. You might think that what you have to say is extremely important and worthy of publication, but a newspaper or magazine only has limited space and if your article is too long it will either be savagely cut or *spiked* (rejected).

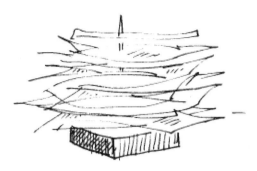

You can also ring newspapers with a comment on something they have published. Ask to speak to the writer concerned and put your views over to him or her. If they're interested in your point of view they might be keen to write a follow up article using you as a source.

How to write a press release

Writing a press release and submitting it to the relevant media is one of the easiest methods of self promotion.

Read newspapers – local and national – and study the style they use. Write your release in the style of the paper you are sending it to. Your release should try to mimic the style of the articles in the paper. For example, if they always print forenames use forenames in your release rather than initials.

In your press release you are trying to imitate the style of the paper. You are also trying to ensure that your release is used rather than one of the hundreds of other releases which are sent to newsrooms up and down the country every day. The content of a release is of paramount importance, but so is the way it is presented. If what you have to say is newsworthy but packaged in completely the wrong way it will stand little chance of publication. However if you have something to say and you write it like a journalist, it stands a good chance of being used.

Newspaper articles do not always follow the rules of English grammar. It has often been said that those whose grasp of the English language is perfect do not necessarily make the best journalists and this is very true. Journalists write in a style which is easily read. Their intention is to catch the reader's eye and then to draw them to the end of the story.

Very few people read all the stories in their morning newspaper. Instead, we tend to look at the headlines and if they interest us we read the first paragraph. If the article still has our attention after the first paragraph we might get further but we rarely reach the end of an article.

So how do journalists attract a reader's attention? They follow some basic rules – the same rules you should follow when writing a press release.

Rules

The rules for writing a press release are:

1 Choose a positive rather than passive headline, i.e. 'Profits Soar at Blogs Brothers' rather than 'Blogs Brothers Announce Annual Results'. Make your headline say something about the story. It should be succinct and give an indication of what is to come.

2 Your first paragraph – the intro or introduction – should be sharp and short; between 12 and 20 words is ideal. Try to convey the main message of the release in the first paragraph.

3 Keep sentences and paragraphs short. Use full stops instead of commas and keep punctuation simple and to a minimum. You do this because readers are less likely to reach the end of long sentences and every punctuation mark acts to break their concentration and can lead to them switching to another story.

4 Avoid superfluous words like 'that' and unnecessary adjectives and adverbs. You don't have to say something is 'marvellous' or 'fantastic'. If it is as good as you claim it is, it will be apparent from the text.

5 Avoid long words. Newspaper columns are narrow. Long words often break over two lines and each hyphenated word means the reader is more likely to lose concentration and switch to another story. If you look at the popular tabloid newspapers you will notice that they rarely have words which are more than ten letters long.

6 Avoid jargon and the use of initials. You might understand the technical terms and what the initials stand for, but the journalist probably won't and the reader won't either.

7   Answer the six Ws – *who, why, what, when, where* and
    how (OK that's not a W but it makes it easier to
    remember). If you don't answer the six Ws your press
    release will not contain all the information a journalist
    needs.

    Who are you writing about?
    Why are you writing about this event?
    What event are you writing about?
    When did it happen?
    Where did it happen?
    How did it happen?

8   Don't write a beginning, middle and end. Put the most
    important points at the beginning of the press release.
    When you reach the end don't summarise, *stop*.
    Newspapers cut articles from the bottom. If an article is
    too long they will cut it from the bottom and if you leave
    your most important point until the end it will never
    make it into print.

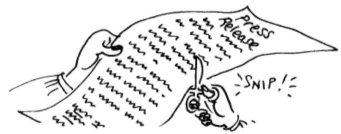

9   Write news not views. What you write should be
    factual. You can include commentary but always
    attribute it to someone and put it in direct quotes.
10 Always double-check the spelling of people's names.
11 Type your press release on one side of the paper only

and in double spacing. Leave a good margin on either side and at the top and bottom of the page so that subbing marks – guidelines for the printers – can be entered later.

12   Always date the release.

13   Always put a daytime contact name and telephone number at the bottom of the release.

14   Keep the release as short as possible – one side of a sheet of paper is best.

'Newspaper speak' vs ordinary English

Consider the following two pieces of news. The first is correct English but it's not written in newspaper style and would stand little chance of being published. The second is an example of how to convey the same message in newspaper style.

Example 1

'The Very Big Company Plc made pre-tax profits of £3.56 million last year. The chairman of the Very Big Company Plc, Sir John Smith, told shareholders at the company's annual general meeting, which was held at the group's headquarters in Barchester, that much of the profit was due to new working practices which had been agreed by the employees. He thanked the employees for their support and said if they had not agreed to the new working practices the Very Big Company Plc would have made a loss. The profits are the largest recorded by the Very Big Company Plc.'

Example 2

> 'The Very Big Company Plc has reported record profits of more than £3.5 million – and it's all thanks to the workforce.
>
> 'Speaking at the company's AGM, chairman, Sir John Smith, said employees' willingness to accept new working practices had turned a potential loss into the company's biggest ever profits.'

When to send the release

Releases can either be sent before an event happens or after it has occurred.

Before the event

If they are sent before the event they can serve as an invitation – informing the journalist that something is due to happen. In many instances it is possible to send out a release a few days in advance but to ensure that nothing is published until after the event has taken place by using an *embargo*.

The embargo is a request to the media to delay publication until the specific date and time stated on the release. In this way journalists are able to write the story in advance which is especially useful if the event is due to take place on a journalist's deadline.

The correct wording for an embargo – which should be printed at the top of the release and on any accompanying documents (annual report, text of speeches, etc.) – is as follows:

'Embargo: Not for release before (time) hours on (day) the (date).'

An embargo for May 4th would therefore read

Embargo: Not for release before 00.01 hours on Monday, May 4th 1992.

One of the best days for getting something printed in daily newspapers is Monday. Journalists on daily newspapers have to work on Sunday on stories for Monday's paper. Many of their traditional sources of information – government, the stock exchange, law courts, etc. – are shut and they therefore rely on people like you to provide them with stories. A 'Sunday for Monday story' should be sent out under embargo the previous Thursday and it should always contain a weekend contact name and telephone number. By doing this the journalist receives the story well in advance, can write it in advance and can contact someone for further information if necessary over the weekend with the story appearing in Monday's paper.

A note of caution – not all journalists will stick to embargoes. Some will break them, so if the information contained in the release is especially sensitive and it would be disastrous if it was printed early – i.e. before you had the chance to tell your staff about impending redundancies, etc. – don't send it out under embargo. Send it after the event.

After the event

If a release is sent out after an event it should be distributed as soon as possible, preferably the same day. News is all about topicality and yesterday's news is quickly old hat. If you can, hand deliver the release to your local press.

Using photography effectively

A picture is worth a thousand words but it is even harder to get a newspaper to use a submitted photo than it is to persuade them to print a press release.

There are two main ways of persuading newspapers to carry photographs.

1 Arrange a photocall – you invite them to send their own photographer to cover an event.
2 Send your own photographs with a press release.

Arranging a photocall

To arrange a photocall you invite newspapers to cover the event. Remember that photographers need good access to the subject. It is no good trying to place them behind a cordon yards away from the action. They need to be able to get up close and to move around freely to get the best angle.

They prefer working in natural light – outdoor shots are always better than indoor – weather permitting.

They need time to take their photos so make sure that those being photographed understand and are prepared to go along with the photographers' requests.

Sending your own photographs

Although many newspapers now carry colour photographs it is still normally better to arrange for your shots to be taken in black and white. If in doubt you can always contact the newspapers concerned to see what they would prefer.

Always use a professional photographer – an amateur, no matter how keen, does not have the experience or the eye for a news angle of a professional. If you don't know any professional photographers, ask the picture desk on your local newspaper who they would recommend. They will normally be happy to supply you with the names of photographers they often use.

Try to think of an interesting angle. Newspapers are swamped with pictures of men in dark suits shaking hands. They've also seen their fair share of outsize cheques being presented for charitable deeds. With a little imagination it is possible to come up with new angles – something which is much more likely to be published.

For instance, instead of having your chairman shaking hands with the chairman of the local football club to publicise a sponsorship deal, why not ask the chairman to kick a ball into the net at the ground. Similarly instead of presenting an outsize cheque representing the proceeds of a sponsored walk or cycle ride, why not have some of the participants literally on their bikes waving fistfuls of fivers or sitting on the ground with their feet up, resting after their labours.

Whatever you decide it is important to have the photographs printed up and distributed as soon as possible after the event – preferably the same day. Photos should be printed up reasonably large (at least 8"x 6") and they should always be captioned. The caption should be attached to the back of the photo by sticky tape so that it can easily be detached without damaging the print. Always include a daytime contact name and phone number on the caption.

Summary

- Anyone can promote themselves
- Use the letters column of your local press
- Use press releases to publicise events
- Always answer the six Ws
- An imaginative picture is worth 1000 words

Action for the day

Decide what you are qualified to comment on.

- What subject areas are you involved in?
- What is your speciality?

Interviews

Radio and television interviews can be nerve-wracking but with a little planning they can be one of the most effective means of self-promotion. Today we shall look at how radio and television interviews are conducted and outline the basic rules and tips for a successful interviewee.

- The radio interview
- The television interview
- Rules and tips

The radio interview

Journalists working for a radio station should be treated in exactly the same way as journalists from a newspaper. They also have deadlines, have to report on stories they know little about and rely on people like you to make their jobs easier.

If you are interested in being interviewed on a local radio station you should aim to make contact with the relevant journalist or programme producer, following the rules laid out on Tuesday. Most radio journalists and producers are keen to hear from potential interviewees. They have many hours of programmes to fill, typically with short, sharp interviews interspersed with music.

This type of programming demands an enormous number of interviews and that's where you come in.

You are the expert whose opinions are of interest to the listeners. You might be able to give your own views on the current economic climate, the unemployment situation in your local town, why your company shuts for the whole of August, why you have chosen to support a particular local charity or any other topic which you believe you have a view on – one which you wish your organisation to be associated with and to gain positive publicity from.

There are two types of radio interview – the one you have initiated yourself and the one in which you are asked to partake.

If you have initiated the interview yourself you will be very much in control of the situation. You have come to the studio to talk about a topic which you have chosen, not to be grilled by a hostile interviewer.

However, if you have been asked to take part in a programme it is a very different story.

Although it is flattering to be invited, you don't have to accept. You should ask yourself if you have anything to gain by taking part in the programme. For example:

- Will the interview be friendly?
- Will you be allowed to put your views across or will the interviewer be trying to put you in a bad light?
- Is the subject really something which you are able to speak confidently on or is it on the fringe of your expertise?

Before agreeing you need to find the answer to the following questions.

- Will the interview be taped or live?
- Who else is taking part – are they hostile or friendly?
- If it is a discussion programme with audience participation, how has the audience been chosen?
- How long is it likely to last?
- What line will the questioning take?
- Is a phone-in involved?

Taped or live?

Although nerve-wracking, live interviews are best because you know that whatever you say will be broadcast. But, with live interviews, if you make a mistake there is no way of correcting it. Taped interviews are easier, but they can be edited, with words and sentences left out so that the final tape might bear little resemblance to what you actually said during the interview. However, if you make a complete hash of a taped interview or find yourself being led into a set of questions you don't want to answer you can always ask the interviewer to change the line of questioning, or ask to answer a particular question again. This is particularly useful if you are one of those people who, when confronted with a large microphone, suddenly find their brain in neutral while their mouth remains in gear.

DID I SAY THAT ?!?

Who else is taking part?

Radio (and television) interviews thrive on controversy.
People don't want to listen to bland statements from
individuals, instead they want to hear heated discussion
between people of differing views. Good interviewers like to
provoke confrontations, so it is important to know who else
will be taking part in the programme.

For instance, if you are asked to talk about the economy you
might find that you have a trade unionist in the chair
opposite you and that you will be expected to defend the
government's record – something you might not be at all
prepared to do.

How has the audience been chosen?

- Has it been picked at random?
- Do members of the audience apply for tickets
  themselves or have they been selected because they
  are likely to oppose what you are going to say and
  therefore provoke a good debate?

How long is it likely to last?

Most radio interviews last for just a few minutes, often
filling in the gaps between records. However some form
much larger programmes – thirty minutes or more. It is
important to know how long you will be expected to talk so
that you can prepare yourself thoroughly.

What line will the questioning take?

It is unlikely that the interviewer will tell you the questions he or she will ask but you may get an idea of the subject area. The interviewer will be just as anxious as you that it should be a good interview and will not want you on the programme if the subject area is outside your knowledge and you will therefore be unable to answer the questions.

Is a phone-in involved?

The phone-in is popular on radio. It enables members of the public to question interviewees and provides the station with listener participation and feedback. If there is a phone-in you will need to prepare yourself even more thoroughly so that you have answers to all the questions which you think you could be asked. Ask one of your colleagues to think up some questions and to give you a grilling beforehand as preparation for the programme.

Phone-ins can be used to your advantage. You can arrange for some of your friends or colleagues to ring the programme with planted questions which you will be able to answer confidently.

The interview itself

Treat the interview as you would one with a newspaper reporter. Do your homework and prepare your answers before you go to the studio.

You should approach the interview with two or three key points which you want to put across. If you will feel more confident, jot these points down on a piece of paper which you can refer to during the interview. Don't attempt to put across more than two or three points – there won't be time and you will end up being rushed and none of the points you were hoping to make will come over clearly.

Try to ignore all the equipment – large microphone, flashing lights, etc. Just concentrate on answering the questions put to you. Do listen to any technical information you are given and, once you are in position, don't move. You will have been wired up for sound and the correct levels set and if you move you will upset these levels with the result that you will either be too faint to be heard or much too loud.

Radio interviews by phone

Treat these just as you would if you were in a studio. Arrange to take the phonecall in a quiet office and post someone outside the door to keep people quiet. During the interview just concentrate on the person on the other end of the telephone. Don't be put off by the voice disappearing to be replaced by music – you are plugged in to what is being broadcast and you are only hearing what members of the audience are picking up on their radios.

Try to avoid coughing, shuffling pieces of paper or anything which will make a sound which will be picked up by the microphones.

If you are asked to say a few words so the sound level can be adjusted say something bland like what you had for breakfast. Don't try to say anything clever or funny – remember the mess Ronald Reagan got himself into when he said the signal had gone out to start bombing the USSR!

The television interview

This is the most nerve-wracking interview of all but it should be approached in the same way as all the others. Thorough preparation is the key.

Television interviews rely on confrontation and a good journalist will be trying to make his or her name as a good chairman by getting opposing views from interviewees.

Bear this in mind before deciding to accept an invitation to appear on television. Answer the same questions as detailed in the radio interview before making your decision.

Before an interview you may well be rung by different researchers for information about what you are going to say. Make sure you say the same thing to each one. Beware the nice sounding young girl – she's probably a hard-nosed and extremely ambitious researcher who is trying to get you to reveal something which could be used against you in the interview.

When you are preparing for the interview, there are several things which need attention:

- What to expect
- What to wear
- The interview itself

What to expect

At the television studio you will probably be shown into the *green room* – the hospitality room – and offered alcoholic refreshment. Do not partake liberally. If you want an alcoholic drink, allow yourself just one. Studio lights have the tendency to make your face go red and if you have more than one glass you could end up looking like a hardened drinker. Alcohol also impairs the brain and will slow your reactions – you need quick wits on television.

In the studio there may well be several cameras and lots of busy people shouting instructions. Try to ignore all this. Concentrate on the interviewer and any fellow guests. Make sure you are comfortable in your seat. Sit well back in your seat with your bottom at the back of the chair – if you lean forward you tend to look shifty and if you relax back into the chair you will look too casual. Keep your elbows on the arms of the chair – this will enable you to move your lower arms for expression but will prevent you from doing an impression of a windmill on camera.

If you are not comfortable, tell someone. If you need to go to the lavatory or want a drink of water, tell someone. It is essential to be comfortable before the programme begins and nerves often lead to a dry mouth and a desire to go to the lavatory.

Once you are in position, stay in it. As in a radio interview you will have been wired up for sound and the cameras will also have been positioned around you. If you move around you could find yourself moving in and out of shot and in and out of focus.

What to wear

Wear something you are comfortable in. You should avoid:

- Black and white – a dark suit with a white shirt provides

too much contrast. Pastel colours work best on television.

- Horizontal stripes – they cause a strobe effect.
- Ties with a strong geometric pattern – for the same reason.
- Very flashy jewellery – the camera and lights will pick it up and it will distract from what you are saying.
- Photochromic glasses – under studio lights they will go very dark and could make you look like a gangster.
- Very tight clothing – the studio lights will make you very warm.

When you are wired for sound, the wire is likely to have to be passed underneath your clothing, which is another reason for avoiding anything too tight. Look at what newsreaders and presenters wear – they're the professionals, so imitate them.

The interview itself

Before the interview starts ask the interviewer what the first question is going to be. This gives you time to prepare your answer.

Concentrate on the interviewer and the questions you are being asked. Do not look at the camera or try to work out if you are on screen – leave that to the cameramen. Answer the questions briefly and try to put across the points you want to make. If you find it hard to concentrate try to imagine that you are talking to someone you know – your mother, husband, wife, etc. Keep your replies simple and avoid using jargon which only you will understand. Don't fiddle with a pen or piece of paper.

Correct any factual inaccuracies straight away, before you start to answer the question.

Act naturally, move your arms if you want to and use facial expressions. Remember the camera could be on you even when you are not answering a question so if someone says something you disagree with shake your head or make some other negative gesture. Gestures like this make good television and you may well find that the camera prefers to focus on you than the person answering the question.

Beware of trick questions – the most famous example being 'When did you stop beating your wife?' to which there is no correct answer. The interviewer always has the last word and can use it to make you look foolish or to put across a point of view which is alien to you right at the end of the programme, when you don't have the opportunity to reply. There is no instant solution for this, but experience will help you to avoid falling into the trap.

At the end stay in your place until you are told to move by the studio manager. Remember you could still be on air.

Television interviews on home ground

Some producers will want to conduct an interview at your office instead of at the studio. Beware of how they might try to present your surroundings. If they want to film the interview outside try to interest them in filming a positive image of your company rather than having an interview with shots of your company rubbish bins or a messy distribution area in the background.

Similarly if the interview is taking place in your office insist that it should be as natural as possible. Try to prevent them from moving all the furniture around – although they will probably have to move some of it. Avoid being filmed with your back to the window as this puts your face in shadow and can lead to you looking shifty.

Again post someone outside the door and arrange to have your telephone re-routed so you won't be disturbed.

Rules and tips

1 Be prepared – always ensure you know the answers to the six Ws.
2 Don't accept an invitation just because you are flattered to be asked – only accept if the interview is going to be worthwhile for you.
3 Ignore the high tech equipment – just concentrate on the interviewer and the questions you are being asked.
4 Wear something comfortable.
5 Go into the interview with two or three points you want to make – and make them. The audience will not remember a larger number of issues. You must answer the question but you should ensure you get your arguments across.
6 Act naturally, don't try to be something you're not.

Summary

- Thorough preparation is essential
- Treat all invitations for radio and TV interviews with caution
- Concentrate on the interviewer – ignore the equipment
- Aim to put across two or three main points

Action for the day

Watch a current affairs programme and listen to how the interviewees handle questions.

- Do they answer the questions they are asked or do they just press ahead with the points they want to make? Which is best?
- What makes 'interesting' television?
- What are they wearing?

Bad publicity

News is something that someone, somewhere doesn't want printed.

The above applies to bad news at least. Today we shall look at what can be done to minimise the effects of bad publicity; how to handle bad news; crisis management; and how to have a correction printed.

- Coping with bad publicity
- Damage limitation
- Handling bad news
- Crisis management
- Corrections

Coping with bad publicity

Although we may want only to present good news to the public we can't control everything that happens or prevent the press from discovering when something has gone wrong. However, contacts that you have made with journalists by following the steps outlined on Tuesday will help you minimise the damage caused by bad publicity.

What to do when bad news strikes

Be prepared. If your workforce has gone on strike, your company has discharged a pollutant into a local river or your financial accountant has disappeared with the weekly pay packets you can bet that the press will hear about it. There is no point in just crossing your fingers and hoping that everything will blow over – it won't and the better prepared you are, the more likely it is you will be able to restrict the damage done.

First, ascertain the facts. Find out exactly what has happened – use the six Ws to ensure you have covered every angle.

Second, brief those staff who need to know. Work out who will talk to the press, will it be you, your chief executive, chairman or someone else – ideally it should only be one person – and make sure they have all the facts they need. Don't forget to brief the telephonist/receptionist, who will be the first point of contact for journalists.

Jot down the facts you are prepared to give out and make sure that anyone else who will deal with the press has the same facts at hand.

Be ready to take calls from the press at anytime. Stories have a habit of breaking outside office hours so be prepared to be called at home. Journalists are very good at discovering home telephone numbers even if they are ex-directory. Ensure that anyone who is likely to answer the telephone – at work or home – knows where to find you and can put the journalist through straight away.

Sometimes it is worth calling the press yourself, to make sure they have your side of the story, for instance if an employee who has been sacked and has a grievance is spreading rumours about the company. Using the contacts you have built up by following the steps outlined on Tuesday you can put the record straight and your prompt action might even nip the story in the bud and prevent it from being printed.

What to do when the journalist calls

If you are not ready, stall for time. Say you are in a meeting, take a note of the journalist's name, newspaper, telephone number and deadline and say you will call back in ten minutes – or however long it will take you to prepare your answers. Make sure you do ring back promptly. All journalists work to deadlines and if you miss the deadline you could find the story printed with no comment or explanation from you and you will have lost the opportunity to put your case forward.

Similarly if the journalist arrives on your doorstep before you are ready, stall for time. Invite him or her in, show him or her to a waiting room and then prepare yourself.

When talking to the journalist try to find out how much he or she knows. Don't volunteer information, wait to be asked. In this way, you can sometimes keep certain items of information out of the press.

A headmistress of an exclusive girls' school was able to keep a potentially scandalous story out of the press by only answering the questions put to her by the journalist. Three of her girls had been caught smuggling boys into their dormitory after attending a party without permission in the local town. They had subsequently been expelled. The local paper heard about the expulsions and the journalist's first question was 'Were drugs involved?' The headmistress was able to put her hand on her heart and swear that wasn't the case and that the girls had broken the rules by attending a party without permission. The journalist didn't think to ask about boys and the news never leaked out.

How to find out how much a journalist knows

You can suggest you talk around the subject. By doing so you can discover how much they really know and how much is guesswork. Don't give any information away, let the journalist do the talking.

Correct any factual inaccuracies immediately

Stick to the facts and the statement you have prepared. If the journalist persists with a line of questioning you are not prepared to answer, tell him or her so but give an explanation – maybe you have to wait until you have the results of an internal enquiry. At all times be polite and courteous; after all the journalist is just doing his or her job.

Damage limitation

Issue a press release which states your side of the story. Make it short and sharp. It should answer the six Ws and it should include a contact name and phone number for outside office hours, as well as during the day.

Inform your superiors – the chairman, board directors, etc.

Inform your employees. They need to know what is going on and it is better that it comes from you rather than from the local paper. Remember, they are ambassadors for your company and they will be talking to their families, friends and neighbours about what has happened. It is better that they know the company line rather than relying on gossip and hearsay.

You should also consider informing your shareholders if the matter is serious. By doing so they will be reassured that the situation is under control and that their investment is safe.

Handling bad news

Bad news should be treated in the same way as good news. Don't try to cover things up, it is much better that you present an honest picture. Don't try to apportion blame or to pass responsibility onto someone else.

How many cases can you recall that have been reported in the national press and on television where the company representative has ended up looking shifty because he or she tried to apportion blame? In too many instances – plane and train crashes, accidents at sea, oil spills, etc – companies are loathe to accept responsibility, preferring to blame the weather, other people, freakish circumstances or even an act of God, when in reality it has been caused by bad management practices.

It is much better to act like Sir Michael Bishop of British Midland who, after the M1 plane crash, went to the scene, promised he would look into the matter and didn't make up feeble excuses. As a result he and the company came across as responsible and caring.

Pick an appropriate press spokesman. This might be your chairman or your managing director, or if they are not at ease handling the press pick another senior executive who is. It is important that whoever you choose should possess the following qualities:

- Confidence when dealing with the media
- Ability to think on their feet and react to questions instantly
- Discretion
- Tact
- Authority

Above all they should be available at all times.

Crisis management

The best form of crisis management is thorough preparation. Plan for a crisis before it occurs. Consider all the things that could go wrong – a fire, theft, strike, accident, etc – and plan your response accordingly. Brief other employees so that they know what to do in an emergency. Write your action plans down so everyone has access to them.

In this way when something does occur you will already have an action plan to put into operation.

Carry out rehearsals in the same way that you carry out fire drills. Test your action plans, make sure they work before you have to use them for real.

In a crisis effective communication is of paramount importance. Communication with the media, the general public, your colleagues, employees and shareholders. Each audience needs to be kept informed. Ways of communicating with each target group should be included in your action plan.

Corrections

What happens if an inaccurate article has appeared in the press and you believe a correction is necessary?

Firstly think long and hard before contacting the paper. Is the inaccuracy really that important? Will a printed correction only keep the story fresh in people's minds? Remember that today's newspaper is tomorrow's fish and chip wrapping and although you might feel aggrieved the chances are that the general public will not remember the article for more than a few days.

If it is a minor error – a misspelling of a name or something similar – it is best to ignore it, but if it is a more serious error – a claim that your profits last year were £1 instead of £1 million, for example – it is worth asking for a correction.

If after consideration, and talking it over with colleagues, you believe a correction is in order you should write to the editor pointing out the inaccuracy and asking what will be done about it. Hand deliver or send the letter by recorded delivery so that you know it has been received by the paper.

Give the editor a reasonable time – two weeks or so – to reply. If at the end of this period you have not received a reply, or you have received an unsatisfactory reply, write again stating that if you do not receive a reply this time you will take the matter further.

You have two options – to go to the Press Complaints Commission or to start legal proceedings against the newspaper.

The Press Complaints Commission

The Press Complaints Commission is an independent body which monitors the standard of the press. However it has no legal authority and it cannot force newspapers to abide by its decisions or print apologies. The Broadcasting Complaints Commission performs a similar role for the broadcast media.

Legal action

Legal action is very expensive and a lengthy business – some cases take years to come to court. Before taking legal action get some dispassionate advice and don't proceed unless you are at least 90 per cent sure of winning your case. Remember that the course of any legal action can be legitimately printed by newspapers. This will reopen the case and the subsequent publicity may be more damaging than the original article. Consider recent libel cases – in how many cases can you correctly identify the winner and in how many do you just remember the alleged libel? All too often the public will only remember the alleged libel, often believing the allegations to be true even if the jury subsequently decide otherwise.

The libel laws are very complex and too detailed to go into in great detail here. Legal action should be seen as a last resort and it should never be started in the heat of the moment. Give yourself a cooling off period before asking yourself whether it really is worth the expense and effort of taking legal action.

Summary

- Bad news can't be avoided but damage can be limited
- Plan for bad news in advance
- Communicate with your staff, shareholders the public, etc. before they read it in the press
- Put your side of the story across

Action for the day

Prepare a bad news action plan. Think about what could go wrong in your company and prepare your action plan accordingly.

Recap

Over the past six days we have had a whistlestop tour of the world of PR. We have examined what PR is and we have listed the basic steps an individual needs to take in order to run his or her own public relations programme successfully.

Today we shall be recapping much of what has gone before, undertaking some practical exercises and preparing an action plan for the future. We will also look at sources of further information and, for ease of reference, a short glossary is included to help individuals understand some PR and media jargon.

- Practical exercises
- Summary
- Action plan
- Useful addresses
- Glossary

Practical exercises

To undertake a successful public relations programme you need to be able to recognise what makes a good story. You also need to be able to sort out the vital facts from the irrelevant.

We will now attempt to write two press releases – one concerning good news, the other bad – from the following information. The facts are in no particular order and they are not all relevant to the story. In each case you should use them to construct a 100 word press release for the *Barchester Echo*, your local paper.

Remember to answer the six Ws as outlined on Wednesday.

You should also remember to put the facts in order of importance, to enable the press release to be cut from the bottom if necessary. Try to make your introduction as interesting as possible.

Good news

- Four of your staff have raised £3196 for charity.
- They raised the money by cycling round the staff car park.

- They completed 2000 laps of the car park between them.
- The money is to be given to the local hospital's (St Peter's) special care baby unit.
- The cheque will be handed over on Friday to the consultant in charge of the unit, Mr Jonathan France.
- The cyclists covered 500 miles during their ride.
- Most of the money raised came from their colleagues at The Very Big Company Plc.
- The Very Big Company Plc's offices are on the Mega Industrial Estate in Barchester.
- The Very Big Company Plc employs 250 people in its Barchester headquarters.
- Your chairman, Sir John Smith MA CBIM, was one of those taking part in the ride. He is 49 and married with three children.
- The other riders were:
  Sheila Jones, Sir John's 21-year-old secretary, who is single.
  Rupert Goodhew, the company's marketing director, who is 39 and divorced with two children.
  Jennifer Cartwright, 35, the company's financial accountant, who is married to Peter Cartwright, headmaster of Barchester High School. They have no children.
- Rupert suffered from blisters on his hands during the cycle ride but completed his 500 laps.

There is no totally right way of writing a press release because everyone has a different style of writing. However the following is an example of a newsworthy release.

BARCHESTER EMPLOYEES
RAISE £3196 FOR CHARITY

Four Very Big Company employees have literally got on their bikes to raise more than £3000 for charity. Led by chairman, Sir John Smith, 49, the intrepid four completed 2000 laps – or 500 miles – of the company car park on the Mega Industrial Estate to raise £3196 for the special care baby unit at St Peter's Hospital in Barchester.

The other three cyclists were Sir John's secretary Sheila Jones, 21, marketing director, Rupert Goodhew, 39 and financial accountant Jennifer Cartwright, 35. Most of their sponsorship money was pledged by their fellow employees.

Bad news

- The Very Big Company Plc made a loss of £2.3 million in the last year.
- The loss was due to the collapse of trade with the USA.
- High exchange rates and the strength of the US dollar affected the company badly.
- The Very Big Company Plc manufactures widgets and is the largest manufacturer of widgets in the UK.
- It employs 250 people at its Barchester headquarters, and a further 3000 at sites throughout the UK.
- Due to the poor results 300 people are being made redundant – 20 from the Barchester offices and the rest from elsewhere in the group.
- It is hoped that most of the redundancies will be voluntary or through natural wastage.
- The redundancies are part of a restructuring package.
- If trade does not pick up, further redundancies might have to be made.
- The redundancies are spread across the board.
- The chairman, Sir John Smith MA CBIM, has blamed the recession and high interest rates for the poor results but is hopeful that the worst is over and that the situation will improve over the next 12 months.

THE WORST IS OVER FOR THE VERY BIG COMPANY

The collapse of trade with the American market has led to the Very Big Company Plc reporting a loss in the last year, but the worst is over according to chairman, Sir John Smith.

The group made a loss of £2.3 million in the last 12 months and is to undergo a restructuring exercise to improve profitability. Three hundred of the company's 3250 jobs are to be lost – most through natural wastage and voluntary redundancy.

Only 20 of the 300 staff at the Barchester headquarters are to lose their jobs.

Sir John Smith said: 'High interest rates and the recession have also contributed to the poor results but we are confident the worst is over.'

Summary

Successful public relations depends on two vital areas – *communication* and *preparation*.

Communication

The ability to communicate coherently with a range of different audiences is of paramount importance. To communicate effectively you need to define your target audiences and to ensure that the right message is tailored for each one. The right message for shareholders is not necessarily the same as the right message for employees and this must be taken into account when you are planning your public relations programme.

Preparation

Thorough preparation is also vital. You should never talk to a journalist or go into an interview without first knowing the answers to the six Ws.

Always ask yourself if a media interview will be worthwhile before accepting. Find out exactly what the interviewer wants from you and don't accept unless you are confident that you will be able to handle the interview and that you will be presented in a positive light.

Action plan

1 Define what subjects you are competent to comment on.
2 Carry out basic market research to find out about your company's current reputation.
3 Compare and contrast different newspaper styles.
4 Define your target audiences.
5 Identify the target media for each separate audience.
6 Prepare a background briefing paper on your company for journalists.
7 Introduce yourself to the relevant journalist on each targeted publication, radio or television station.
8 Study the television professionals and learn from them.
9 Prepare action plans for possible bad news stories.
10 Keep a scrapbook of all your newspaper cuttings so that you can see at a glance just what you have achieved.

Remember that the effects of a planned and sustained public relations programme are not instantaneous. Instead media contacts are built up over a period of time. Mutual trust and confidence between public relations officers and journalists is not gained overnight.

No matter how well written a press release is or how newsworthy you think the subject is, not everything that you write will be published. In fact a great deal of what you circulate will never see the light of day in a newspaper.

With this in mind restrict what you send out. Don't send a release just because you haven't sent one for a while and it seems about time the press heard from you again. Always wait until you have something worthwhile to say. If the press receive non-newsy releases from you they will begin to think that all your press releases are irrelevant. You will then be in danger of having your releases binned before the journalist has time to read them properly.

If you have been sending out regular releases but don't feel that you have much to show for it in your scrapbook, don't be too disheartened. Public relations activity can be likened to a dripping tap, each drip on its own makes little impression but taken together the drips will eventually leave their mark.

Useful addresses

Media contacts

There are many directories which list all the newspapers and magazines published in the UK together with details of television and radio stations. They should be available in your local library.

Among the best known are

PR Planner

Media Information Limited
Hale House
290-6 Green Lanes
London N13 5TP

Pims Directories

Pims House
Mildmay Avenue
London N1 4RS

Blue Book of British Broadcasting

Tellex Monitors Limited
Communications House
210 Old Street
London EC1V 9UN

Some companies will arrange to mail your press releases for you, for a fee.

Among the best known of these is:

Two Ten Communications

210 Old Street
London EC1V 9UN

Public relations and PR consultancies

Institute of Public Relations (IPR)

The Old Trading House
15 Northburgh Street
London EC1V 0PR

Public Relations Consultants Association (PRCA)

Willow House
Willow Place
Victoria
London SW1P 1JH

Hollis Press and Public Relations Annual

Contact House
Lower Hampton Road
Sunbury-on-Thames
Middlesex TW16 5HG

The above list is for guidance only and is by no means
exhaustive. It should not be taken as a recommendation and
individuals should contact more than one organisation
before making a decision about which is most suitable for
their situation.

Glossary

Copy   A written story for a newspaper or magazine.

Embargo   The date and time at which a news item may be publicised.

Go to bed   The time at which the press is prepared for printing.

Intro   The first paragraph of a newspaper article.

Spiked   A story which has been rejected.

Splash   The main story on a newspaper page.

Sub   The sub-editor of a newspaper, responsible for page layout, headlines, etc.